D1650540

BASIL TAP DANCING

by
Diana Washbourne A.N.A.T.D., S.B., A.T.B.

The photographs show
Sue Protheroe   Debbie Blake
and other students
of the
GLENLYN STAGE & BALLET SCHOOL
Forest Hill, London

CONTENTS

FOREWORD

I am sure not only pupils, but teachers also, will enjoy the knowledge to be gained from studying this book by Diana.

She is a school teacher as well as the Principal of one of the largest stage schools in South East London.

This book is the result of her extensive teaching experience - it is very modern in its outlook, incorporating good technique and helping to build up various rhythms so essential to Tap Dancing, a very creative art.

Ruby Diggens

F.N.A.T.D., M.I.D.T.A.
Examiner - Adjudicator
British Federation of Musical Festivals

DEBBIE and SUE SHOW YOU HOW TO TAP

INTRODUCTION

There is a great deal of pleasure and joy to be gained from watching, but even more from learning how to, dance. From a very early age young children respond to music, moving freely and expressively.

Tap dancing can be enjoyed by boys and girls of all age groups: it is not necessary to start learning whilst a youngster. You will find it fascinating and, what's more important, FUN at any age.

If you take a structured course at a recognised school of dancing you will be given the opportunity to take examinations in one or more of the dance associations, and probably a chance to show your talents and acquired skills to others by appearing in displays and other entertainments.

This little book will introduce you to the basic steps of tap dancing and gives you practices to do at home. It is NOT a substitute for a good teacher but will, we hope, encourage you to go on and learn more.

DRESS

You will feel more like dancing, and certainly feel more free to move, if you are dressed correctly and smartly.

If you have long hair, tie it back or wear it up so that it doesn't flap around your face.

Remember to hold yourself well, even when practising. Dancers are usually recognisable by their good poise.

Try not to look down at your feet

If you have a full-length mirror, you can use it to see your faults and correct them.

Fig. 1. Leotards and tights are best

When practising it is particularly important to feel warm and comfortable, but also to be free to move in any direction. Leotards and thick tights are best, but you could wear leg-warmers if you are practising at home, or slacks or a track suit especially in cold weather.

Most good sport shops, and several chain stores, stock suitable dance wear, and in many towns there are dance boutiques which specialise in dance wear items.

Fig. 2. Slacks for practising at home

Fig. 3. Keep your legs warm

Fig. 4. Keep warm after dancing

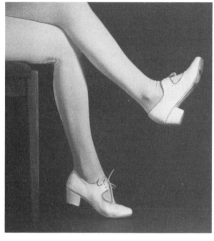

Fig. 5. Make sure your shoes fit well

SHOES

A pair of good flexible shoes is essential, and most dance equipment shops will be pleased to advise you. For men and boys, lace-up Oxfords are best but these are expensive and an alternative would be a pair of light-weight shoes to which toe-taps have been added.

For a girl, a pair of Oxfords is most suitable but many prefer a shoe with a bar across fastening with a bow of ribbon or laces on the instep (known as 'American Bow-tie'), or the popular character shoes.

Some prefer a silver or gold party sandal to which taps have been added. Slingbacks are definitely not suitable, because it is important that the shoes grip your heel firmly.

Heeltaps give a better tone to some heel actions but are not necessary in the early stages. Jingle taps

which rattle as if loose do not enhance the sounds, and are not allowed in examinations.

Before buying, test the shoes as follows: sit down, place your feet flat on the floor and bend the toe joints, lifting your heels as far as possible off the floor. If the soles bend easily and the shoes do not pinch or slip off your feet – buy them. Do *not* pick up a pair of shoes and bend them in half by hand as this proves nothing and can damage the shoes.

Fig. 6. Toe tap fitted
Fig. 7. Four types of shoe

TIME, TEMPO and RHYTHM

To be able to tap dance well, you must have an understanding of time, tempo and rhythm. Begin by clapping and walking in time to music, and the idea of the rhythm of tap with the feet will follow.

TIME is the *beat* of the music,
        like the steady ticking of a clock.
TEMPO is the *speed* at which it is played.
RHYTHM is the *musical pattern* made by dividing up the beat within the time signature. You can create many varied, unusual and interesting rhythms once you have mastered the basics.

Fig. 8. This is a 4-bar phrase of $\frac{4}{4}$ time

$\frac{4}{4}$ Time is the most common time signature. It is counted 1 2 3 4 5 6 7 8 , four beats to each bar of music. You do not need to be able to read music to tap dance, but this shows how music is arranged in 'bars'.

Practice

Clap your hands and snap your fingers to mark the beats. Try this to music, saying the words 'one, two, three, four, etc' as you clap and wait, keeping a steady rhythm.

Note: The crossed figures, ie 5̷ 6̷ 7̷ 8̷, always indicate a 'wait' or 'pause'.

Clap four beats	1 2 3 4
Wait four beats	5̷ 6̷ 7̷ 8̷
Clap four beats	1 2 3 4
Wait four beats	5̷ 6̷ 7̷ 8̷

That is a 4-bar phrase.

Now practise these four bars:

Clap four beats	1 2 3 4
Clap snapfingers	5 6
Clap snapfingers	7 8
Clap four beats	1 2 3 4
Clap snapfingers	5 6
Clap snapfingers	7 8

Remember to keep a steady rhythm all the time.

When you can do this, vary the rhythm
in the second and fourth bars by doing
TWO quick claps for every beat:

Clap four beats   1   2   3   4   (1st bar)

Clapclap clapclap clapclap clapclap
                  &5   &6   &7   &8   (2nd bar)
Clap four beats   1   2   3   4   (3rd bar)

Clapclap clapclap clapclap clapclap
                  &5   &6   &7   &8   (4th bar)

Now practise this 8-bar combination:
Clap	1	2	3	4
Clapclap	&5	&6	&7	&8
Clap	1	2	3	4
Clap	5			
Wait	6̶			
Clap	7			
Wait	8̶			

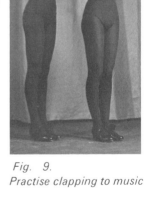

Fig. 9.
Practise clapping to music

Repeat these four bars.
Practise these exercises until you can keep up a steady time.

Fig. 10. This is a 4-bar phrase of $\frac{3}{4}$ time

Another usual time signature is $\frac{3}{4}$ time, or waltz time, having three beats to each bar.

Try clapping these four bars:

Clap	1	2	3
Clap	4	5	6
Clap	1	2	3
Clap	4	5	6

Now vary the rhythm and clap these four bars:

Clap wait wait   1 2 3
Clap wait wait   4 5 6

Repeat

When you can do that easily, try:

Clap clapclap clapclap   1 &2 &3
Clap clapclap clapclap   4 &5 &6
Clap clapclap clapclap   1 &2 &3
Clap clapclap clapclap   4 &5 &6

You can divide each beat into many parts, but in this book we only deal with:

QUARTER NOTES

    — One sound for each beat

EIGHTH NOTES

    — Two sounds for each beat

TWELFTH NOTES

    — Three sounds for each beat

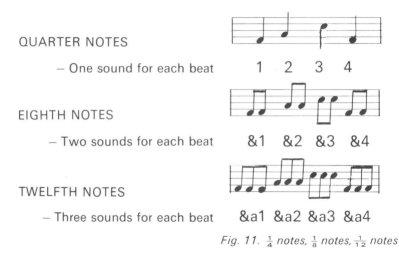

1   2   3   4

&1   &2   &3   &4

&a1 &a2 &a3 &a4

Fig. 11. $\frac{1}{4}$ notes, $\frac{1}{8}$ notes, $\frac{1}{12}$ notes

Practise clapping and saying slowly:

1	2	3	4		1	2	3	4
&5	&6	&7	&8		&a5	&a6	&a7	&a8

MUSIC

FOR

PRACTICE

Here are some well-known tunes:

'Singing in the Rain'
'When the Midnight Choo-Choo leaves for Alabama'
'Happy Days are Here Again'
'Bye, Bye, Blackbird'
'For Me and My Gal'
'The Green, Green Grass of Home'
'Consider Yourself'
'The Entertainer'
'If I were a Rich Man'
'Daisy, Daisy' ($\frac{3}{4}$ time)
'Cruising Down the River' ($\frac{3}{4}$ time)
'I'm just a Girl'
'Surrey with a Fringe on Top'
'If my Friends could see Me now'
'I'm gonna wash that Man right out of my Hair'
Theme song from *'Cabaret'*

Any music with a steady beat is suitable for tap dancing. Most record shops stock instrumental music, of which the piano is most suitable, but it is just as easy to practise whilst singing or humming a tune.

You can use present-day music as long as the rhythm and beat are there, but music from popular shows which have been performed over many years has proved useful.

WARMING-UP

It is very important to warm up your muscles at the beginning of each dance session — this is to get your muscles relaxed and supple.

All professional dancers spend quite a time warming-up before they dance.

1. *Ankle movement.* Hold on to a support. Lift your right foot and point your toe down as far as you can; then point your toe up as far as possible. Move up and down slowly, counting to 8. Then change feet and repeat the exercise with your left foot.

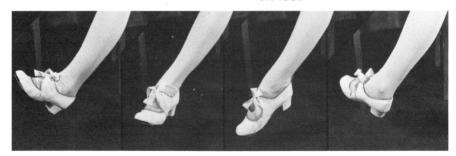

Fig. 12. Ankle circling

2. *Ankle circling.* Many tap steps start from the ankle joint so this is a very important exercise. Hold on to a support. Raise your left leg, pointing your toe upwards and then circle your foot round slowly, counting 1 2 3 4. Do this four times and then circle in the opposite direction. Change to do the same exercise with your right leg.

As a variation, you can combine two slow circles, taking four counts each, with four quick circles taking two counts each.

Now combine the up and down movement with the circling:

Two up and down movements
1 2 3 4

Two quick circles 5 6 7 8

Repeat and then practise with the other leg.

You can do these exercises sitting on a chair.

3. *Walking or skipping to music,* see page 24.

Fig. 13. Young children love skipping to music

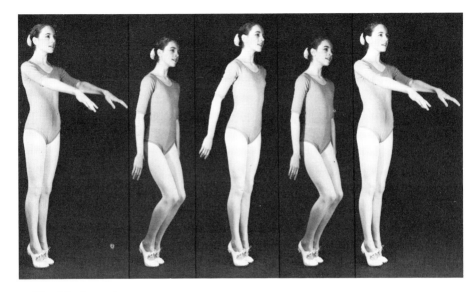

Fig. 14. Bouncing

4. *Bouncing* on the balls of both feet, with the arms swinging freely forward and back. Count 1 2 3 4.

Practice
Four slow bounces taking two counts each 1 2 3 4 5 6 7 8
Then eight quick bounces &1 &2 &3 &4 &5 &6 &7 &8
Then repeat four slow bounces and eight quick.
Remember to stand on the balls of your feet and let your knees relax.

5. *Jumping and clapping,* landing
   on both feet. You can combine
   this with bouncing.

Practice
(a) Two quick bounces &1 &2
    Jump clap   3   4
    Two quick bounces &5 &6
    Jump clap   7   8
    Repeat.

(b) Four slow bounces

                        1 2 3 4
                        5 6 7 8
    Jump clap   1 2
    Jump clap   3 4
    Jump clapclap   5 &6
    Jump clapclap   7 &8

Fig. 15. Jump and clap

Fig. 16. Jump and clap sideways

Try jumping sideways to alter the appearance. Start with feet together.

Slide one foot out to the side and off the ground, at the same time springing off from the other foot. Land with feet together, knees relaxed.

6. *Springing.* Stand on one foot, spring up into the air
and land lightly on the ball of the other foot.
Practice Seven springs from foot to foot and clap.

Springs   1 2 3 4 5 6 7   Repeat.
Clap   8

Practise this combination of jumps and springs:

Two sideways jumps to R & L   1 2 3 4
Lift R leg   5
Three springs R L R   6 7 8   Repeat, starting to L side.

Fig. 17. Springing on the spot

Fig. 18. Hopping

7. *Hopping.* Stand on one foot, spring up into the air
   and land lightly on the ball of the same foot.
   Practice
   Combine hopping and springing:

(a) Spring R, spring L   1 2
    Spring R, hop R   3 4   (b) Three hops, clap   1 2 3   4
    Spring L, spring R 5 6   Two hops spring clapclap 5 6 7 &8
    Spring L, hop L   7 8   Three hops, clap   1 2 3   4
    Repeat.   Two hops spring clapclap 5 6 7 &8

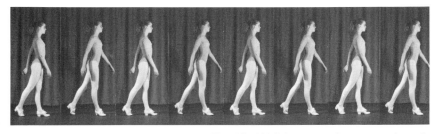

Fig. 19. Walking—one beat to each walk

WALKING

Walking to music is very good practice. It encourages good poise (always remember to hold your head up and 'walk tall'), it develops a sense of time and rhythm, and is also useful as a warming-up exercise. Young children always enjoy marching and skipping to music.

Practice   (a) Eight walks, one walk to each beat, counting:

           1 2 3 4 5 6 7 8
           R L R L R L R L

           Four walks, two beats to each walk, counting:

           1 2 3 4 5 6 7 8
           R   L   R   L

(b) Two walks, one beat each, followed by one walk of two beats,
counting:
```
1 2 3 4 5 6 7 8
R L R   L R L
```

(c) Three walks, two beats each, followed by two walks, one beat each:
```
1 2 3 4 5 6 7 8    1 2 3 4 5 6 7 8
L   R   L   R L    R   L   R   L R
```
You can make up variations for yourself and this will give you
real practice in discovering the variations in the rhythm of tap.

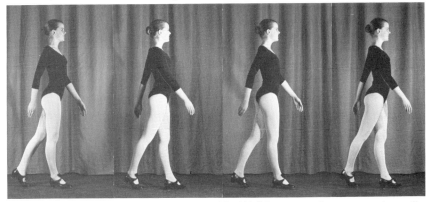

Fig. 20. Walking—two beats to each walk

GALLOPS

These are continuous sideways travelling steps which should be performed lightly on the balls of the feet. Gallops are used in all forms of dance: ballet, modern, country, etc. They are useful in warming-up exercises and little children enjoy galloping in a circle, holding hands.

Practice

(a)

1&	2&	Two gallops to R
3		Step R to R side
4		Close L foot to R
5&	6&	Two gallops to L
7		Step L to L side
8		Close R foot to L

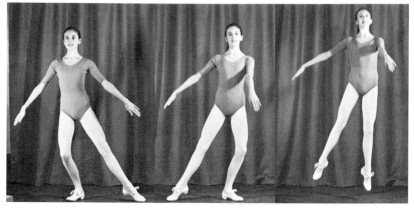

Fig. 21. Gallop

(b)

1& 2& 3&	Three gallops to R	
4	Step R to R side	
5& 6& 7&	Three gallops to L	
8	Step L to L side	
1& 2& 3&	Three gallops to R	
4	Step R to R side	
5	Step L to L side	

6	Close R foot to L
7	Step R to R side
8	Close L foot to R

Repeat starting L.

Later try clicking your heels as they meet in the air. This will add another sound to the gallop.

The next pages show you how to make the different tap sounds with the different parts of your feet. Later you will learn how to link the sounds and movements together to produce an interesting sequence of sound.

But first, practise the steps until you can do them smartly without having to think of every movement you make.

Practise slowly at first, and hold on to a chair so that you don't have to worry about balancing.

Fig. 22. Straight tap

STRAIGHT TAP

Stand on the ball of one foot (called the supporting foot), with your knee relaxed.

Extend the other foot (called the working foot), forward and just off the ground.

Strike the ground sharply with the ball of the working foot and turn the toe up well using just the ankle joint to produce this upward movement. This step should make one clear sound, the metal tap on your shoe making the sound.

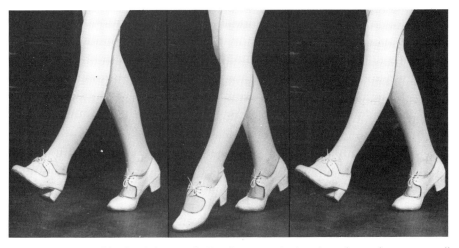

Fig. 23. Straight tap. Strike the ground sharply and turn the toe up well

Practice

Seven straight taps with the R foot   Put it down (Step)

Seven straight taps with the L foot   Put it down

Remember to use the ankle joint fully, and turn up the toe well. Note: the transfer of weight from R foot to L foot, or L foot to R foot, is a STEP, and can be done in any direction.

FORWARD AND BACKWARD TAP

Forward tap

Using a support at first, stand on the ball of one foot, with the working foot lifted up behind. Relax the supporting knee. Strike the ground sharply with the ball of the foot as it moves forward and off the ground.

This tap is produced from the ankle joint, like the straight tap, and the metal tap makes one clear sound.

Fig. 24. Forward tap

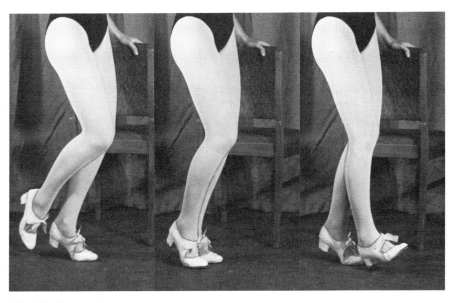

Fig. 25. Forward tap

Backward tap

Stand on the ball of one foot and extend the working foot forward and just off the ground. Strike the ground sharply with the ball of the foot as it moves backwards and off the ground.

Practise a forward and a backward tap together, remembering that the movement must come from the ankle.

(b)

1 2	R forward tap, backward tap
3	Step R
4	Wait
5 6	L forward tap, backward tap
7	Step L
8	Wait

Repeat three times.

Practice

(a) Start with R foot up behind:

1 2	R forward tap, backward tap
3 4	R forward tap, backward tap
5 6	R forward tap, backward tap
7	Step R
8	Wait
1 2	L forward tap, backward tap
3 4	L forward tap, backward tap
5 6	L forward tap, backward tap
7	Step L
8	Wait

Repeat once.

(c)

1 2	R forward tap, backward tap
3	Hop on L foot
4	Step R
5 6	L forward tap, backward tap
7	Hop on R foot
8	Step L

Repeat six times.

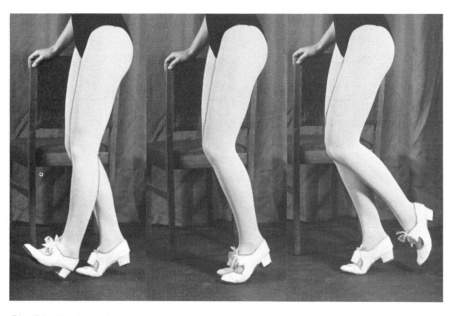

Fig. 26. Backward tap

SHUFFLE

A shuffle is a forward and backward tap combined quickly, making two sounds to one beat.

Instead of counting 1 forward, 2 backward, you must count '&1' (one beat).

Practice

Here are five 4-bar amalgamations.

Practise each until you can do it easily.

(a)

1	Forward tap R	1	Forward tap L
2	Backward tap R	2	Backward tap L
3	Forward tap R	3	Forward tap L
4	Backward tap R	4	Backward tap L
&5	Shuffle R	&5	Shuffle L
&6	Shuffle R	&6	Shuffle L
&7	Shuffle R	&7	Shuffle L
8	Step R	8	Step L

(b)
&1 &2 &3	Shuffle R three times
4	Step R
&5 &6 &7	Shuffle L three times
8	Step L
	Repeat

(c)
1 2 3 4	Four springs R L R L
&5	Shuffle R
6	Step R
&7	Shuffle L
8	Step L
	Repeat

(d)
&1	Shuffle R
2	Step R
&3	Shuffle L
4	Step L
&5	Shuffle R
6	Step R
7	Spring on to L
8	Spring on to R
	Repeat

(e)
&1	Shuffle R
&2	Hop L step R
&3	Shuffle L
&4	Hop R Step L
&5	Shuffle R
6	Step R
&7	Shuffle L
8	Step L
	Repeat

BALL CHANGE

A ball change is another step which makes two sounds to one beat, and is counted '&1'. It is a transfer of weight, stepping on to the ball of one foot and then on to the ball or flat of the other.

Practice

Here are three 4-bar amalgamations to practise.

(b)

1 2 3 4	Spring R L R L
&5 &6 &7	Ball change R L R L R L
8	Step on to R
1 2 3 4	Spring L R L R
&5 &6 &7	Ball change R L R L R L
8	Step on to L

(a)

&1	Ball change R L
&2	Ball change R L
&3	Ball change R L
4	Step forward on R
&5	Ball change L R
&6	Ball change L R
&7	Ball change L R
8	Step forward on L
	Repeat

(c)

&1 &2	Shuffle R, ball change R L
&3 &4	Shuffle R, ball change R L
&5 &6	Shuffle R, ball change R L
7	Step forward on R
8	Finger snap
&1 &2	Shuffle L, ball change L R
&3 &4	Shuffle L, ball change L R
&5 &6	Shuffle L, ball change L R
7	Step forward on L
8	Finger snap

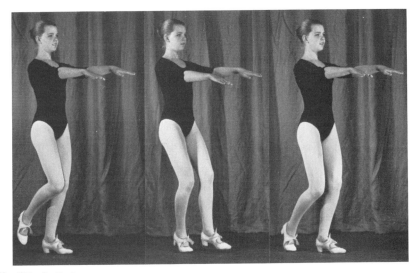

Fig. 27. Ball change

Ball change is usually done from the back foot to the front foot but can be done in any direction, see Fig. 28 over the page. Remember to keep the movements smooth and continuous, and let your arms swing naturally by your sides when practising the amalgamations.

STEP

*Fig. 28. Ball change
—sideways finish*

Fig. 29. Step on to the ball of foot

STEP

This is the transfer of weight from one foot to the ball of the other, and can be in any direction.

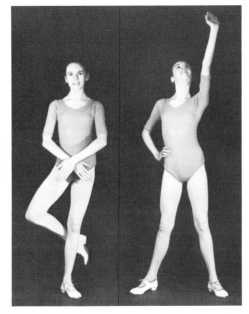

Fig. 30. Stepping sideways on to flat of foot

STAMP

This is a heavy downward beat on to the flat of the foot. The weight may be on the working foot or on the supporting foot. A stamp can be taken in any direction.

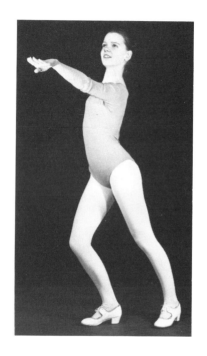

Fig. 31. Stamp—weight on working foot

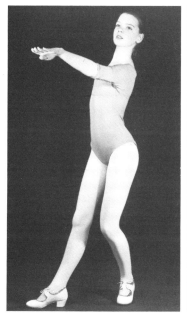

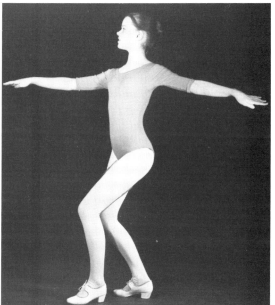

Fig. 32. Stamp
—weight on supporting foot

Fig. 33. Stamp across

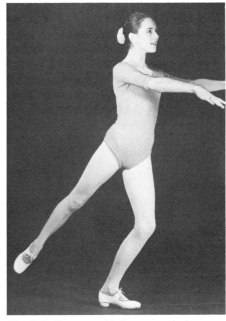

DROP

This is similar to a spring but landing heavily on the ball or flat of the foot, with the other leg lifted behind, straight or bent.

Practice

Here are two 4-bar amalgamations including step, stamp and drop.

(a)

1   Stamp R across L
2   Replace R beside L
3   Stamp L across R
4   Replace L beside R
5   Spring R
6   Spring L
7   Drop on to R
8   Wait

Fig. 34. Drop—with leg extended behind

1   Stamp L across R
2   Replace L beside R
3   Stamp R across L
4   Replace R beside L
5   Spring L
6   Spring R
7   Drop on to L
8   Wait

(b)
1   Stamp R forward
2   Stamp L forward
3   Step R back
4   Step L back
&5 Shuffle R
6   Step R
&7 Shuffle L
8   Step L
    Repeat

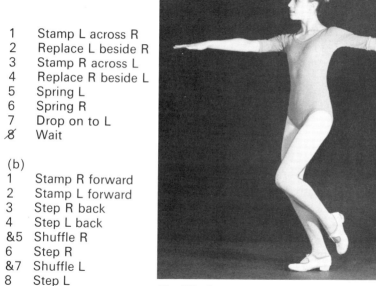

Fig. 35. Drop — on to flat of foot

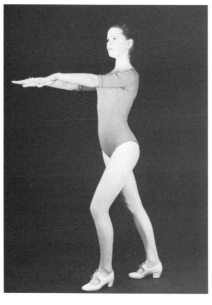

BALL TAP, HEEL TAP, TOE TAP

All 'taps' finish with the foot off the ground and make one clear sound.

Ball tap

Strike the ground with the ball of the foot and lift it up sharply. Ball tap can be done in three ways: Figs: 36, 37, 38.

*Fig. 36. Ball tap—
heel of working foot
on ground
Fig. 37. Ball tap
—standing on one foot*

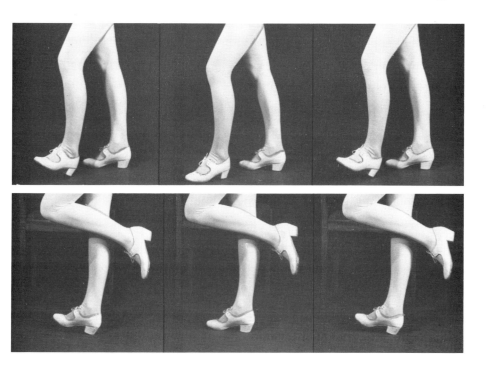

46

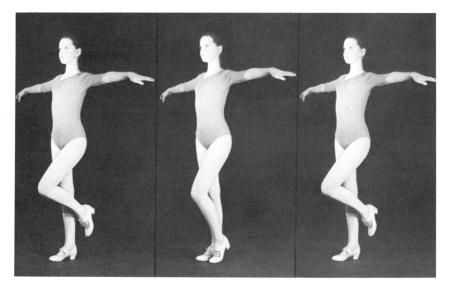

Fig. 38. Ball tap—sharp dig. Strike the ground with ball sharply, and lift

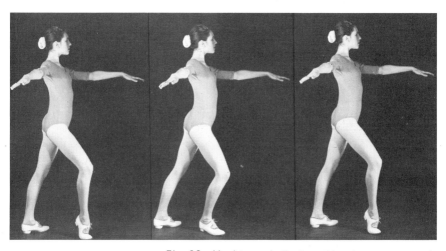

Fig. 39. Heel tap—ball of working foot on ground

Heel tap

Strike the ground with the heel and lift it up sharply.
Heel tap can also be done in three ways:
1. With the ball of the working foot on the ground, Fig. 39 above.
2. As a sharp dig, Fig. 40 (next page).
3. With one foot off the ground, Fig. 41.

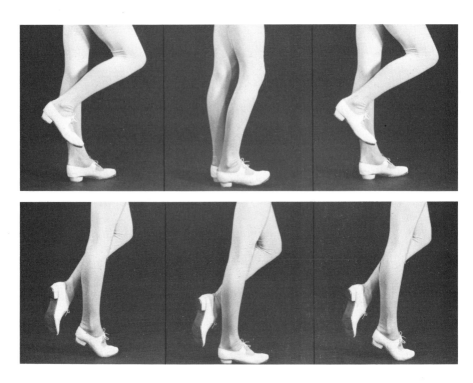

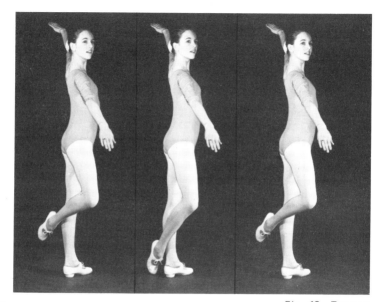

Fig. 40. (top) Heel dig
Fig. 41. (lower) Heel tap
—standing on one foot

Fig. 42. Toe tap

Toe Tap

Lift the working foot behind, strike the ground sharply with the toe and lift again quickly.

BEATS

A beat has one sound produced in the same way as a tap but the foot remains on the ground. This makes a sound heavier in tone.

Practice

Here are four 4-bar amalgamations using taps and beats.

(a)
1		Stamp R
2		Stamp L
3		Step back R
4		Step back L
&5	&6	Shuffle R, hop step
&7	&8	Shuffle L, hop toe tap

1		Stamp L
2		Stamp R
3		Step back L
4		Step back R
&5	&6	Shuffle L, hop step
&7	&8	Shuffle R, hop toe tap

Fig. 43. Ball beat—finish with foot on ground

(b) Remember to step on to the *ball* of your foot.

1	Step R
2	Heel beat R
3	Step L
4	Heel beat L
5	Spring on to R
6	Spring on to L
7	Spring on to R
&8	Toe tap L hop R

1	Step L
2	Heel beat L
3	Step R
4	Heel beat R
5	Spring on to L
6	Spring on to R
7	Spring on to L
&8	Toe tap R, hop L

(c)

1 2 3	Spring R L R
4	Toe tap L
5 6 7	Spring L R L
8	Toe tap R

Repeat

(d)

1	Step forward R
2	Heel beat R
3	Step forward L
4	Heel beat L
5	Step R to R side
6	Ball dig L
7	Step L to L side
8	Ball dig R

Repeat

Fig. 44. Parallel arm position

ARM POSITIONS

The arm positions enhance and add interest to the steps you perform with your feet. It is important that your arm movements co-ordinate with your feet and head, otherwise you will look awkward and unbalanced.

Practise the basic arm positions in front of a mirror until they look and feel right.

These are the basic arm positions:

Parallel

Your arms are straight and the same distance apart. As long as your arms remain parallel they can be at any angle to your body: high, low, extended or shortened (here the arms are bent at the elbow but the lower arms are parallel), Figs. 44 to 47.

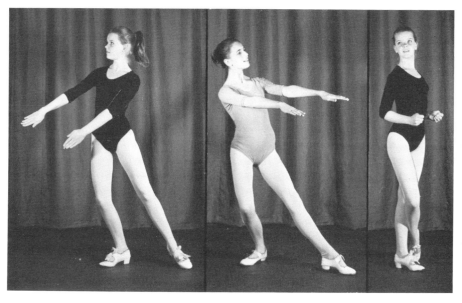

Fig. 45. Low parallel arms

Fig. 46. Extended
parallel arms

Fig. 47
Shortened
parallel arms

Fig. 48. Co-ordinated arms

Fig. 49. Co-ordinated arms—ready to circle both arms together

Co-ordinated

Your arms are moving in the same direction at the same time. Any arms moving together whether across your body, forward and backward, or circling etc., are co-ordinated.

Fig. 50. Horizontal arms—making a right-angle with the body

Fig. 51. Extended horizontal arms

Horizontal

Your arms make a right-angle with your body. Some parallel arm positions are horizontal.

Opposition

As you walk, your arms swing naturally in opposition, i.e., your right foot forward balanced by your left arm. Opposition arms in dance are based on exactly that principle: the right foot balanced by the left arm and the left foot balanced by the right arm, Fig. 52.

Opposition also means that arms are placed in opposite directions, i.e., one forward, one back, or one high, one low. Figs. 53, 55. In dance, the opposition line is extended: try to stretch through your body to your finger tips. Fig. 54.

Practice

Here is a 4-bar amalgamation

Fig. 52. Opposition arms
let your arms
swing naturally

1 2 3	Walk forward L R L
4	Stamp R with weight back
5 6 7	Walk backward R L R
8	Stamp L

Fig. 53.	*Fig. 54.*	*Fig. 55.*
Opposition arms	*Opposition arms*	*Opposition arms*
—arms in	*—extended, stretching*	*—in opposition*
opposite directions	*through to the fingertips*	*to working foot*

1 2	Step forward L, heel beat	⎫ use
3 4	Step forward R, heel beat	⎬ extended
5 6	Step forward L, heel beat	⎪ opposition
7 8	Step forward R, heel beat	⎭ arms

ARMS – MODERN LINES

It is important to remember when tap dancing that all parts of the body, not only the feet, are involved. This includes the arms, the head (eyes are very important), and the body itself.

Generally, the head follows the line of the arms and the eyes are raised along that line looking into the distance. Try to develop your own style from the very beginning because it is your own personality that should show through when you dance. As you become more experienced in co-ordinating your arms with your feet in dancing, experiment and try to discover how you can use your arms and head to express how *you* feel. Figs. 56 to 62 show modern arm lines based on the basic lines, with the dancer's own personality coming through.

Fig. 56. Modern arm lines

Fig. 57.   Fig. 58.

Fig. 59.

Fig. 60.

Fig. 61.

Fig. 62.

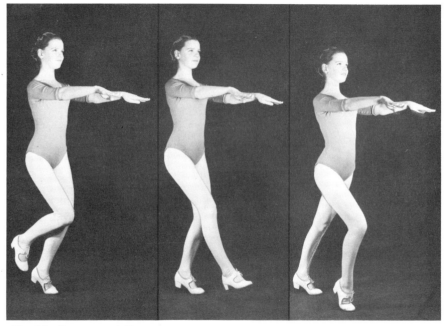

Fig. 63. Tap step—followed by — Fig. 64. Heel beat

Fig. 64. Heel beat

TAP STEP

This is a forward tap followed immediately by a step. This makes two clear sounds which are counted '&1'.

Your weight can be on the front or on the back foot.

Remember to turn your foot up on the forward tap, and finish with a relaxed knee. Practise a tap step followed by a heel beat.

Practices on page 66.

Fig. 65. Tap spring

TAP SPRING

This is a forward tap followed immediately by a spring. This makes two clear sounds and is counted '&1'.

Do not swing your foot too far forward, but try for plenty of elevation (lift). This step should be done very lightly and can be done on one spot, or travelling.

Practise the amalgamations on the following pages.

Practice exercises for **TAP STEP** and **TAP SPRING**

Repeat these amalgamations with arms in opposition to working foot, changing arms as you change your feet.

(a) Tap Step
&1 Tap step R
&2 Tap step L
&3 Tap step R
4 Heel beat R
&5 Tap step L
&6 Tap step R
&7 Tap step L
8 Heel beat L
Repeat

(b) Tap Step
&1 2 Tap step R, heel beat R
&3 4 Tap step L, heel beat L
&5 6 Tap step R, heel beat R
&7 8 Tap step L, heel beat L
Repeat

(c) Tap spring
Practise this 4-bar amalgamation using opposition arms.
&1 Tap spring R
&2 Tap spring L
&3 Tap spring R
&4 Clap clap
&5 Tap spring L
&6 Tap spring R
&7 Tap spring L
&8 Clap clap

&1 Tap spring R
&2 Tap spring L
&3 Tap step R
&4 Ball change LR
&5 Tap spring L
&6 Tap spring R
&7 Tap step L
&8 Ball change RL

Fig. 66. Tap spring

When you are confident and familiar with this last amalgamation add:

(d)

&1	&2	Shuffle R, ball change
&3	&4	Tap step, heel beat R
&5	&6	Shuffle L, ball change
&7	&8	Tap step, heel beat L

&1	2	Tap spring R, finger snap
&3	4	Tap spring L, finger snap
&5	6	Tap spring R, finger snap
&7	&8	Shuffle L, ball change

Then repeat the whole 8-bar amalgamation, starting with three tap springs L R L.

PATTERN AND DIRECTION

This is important when putting steps together in an arrangement.

Pattern is the shape of the work. It is made by the movement of the dancers as they take steps in different directions on the stage.

Direction is the line on which the steps are taken.

The directions of the stage are shown in Fig. 67. Remember that the directions never alter: you move according to the directions of the stage. It is best at first to practise everything to the front.

To gain confidence in the use of different directions, practise just walking and turning. When turning from one direction to another it is usual to turn *away* from the supporting foot, see Figs. 68 and 69.

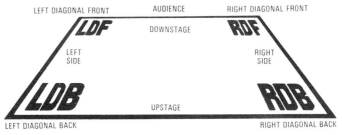

Fig. 67. Stage directions   LDF – *Left diagonal front*   RDF – *Right diagonal front*
LDB – *Left diagonal back*   RDB – *Right diagonal back*

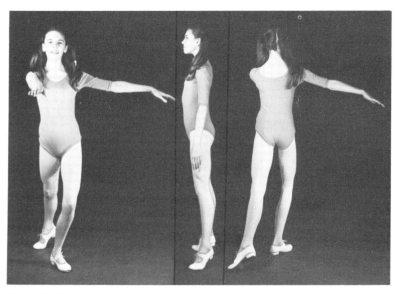

Fig. 68. Turning—$\frac{1}{2}$ turn to right

Practice

(a) Stand in the centre, facing RDF.
   Use opposition arms, start with R foot.

1 2 3 4	Four walks to RDF
5 6 7 8	Pivot on L foot, start on R foot, four walks to LDB
1 2 3 4	Start R foot, four walks to front
5 6 7 8	Start R foot, three walks to back, dig L

   Repeat starting L foot, walking to LDF.

(b) Start facing RDF.

&1 &2	Tap step R, ball change
&3 &4	Tap step L to LDF, ball change
&5 &6 &7 &8	Four tap springs to LDF, R L R L
1	Step forward R to LDF
2	Turn on balls of feet to RDB
&3 &4	Shuffle ball change R
5 6	Face back. Step to L side (of stage) on R foot. Close L foot to R foot
7 8	Step R, dig L.

   Repeat, starting facing RDB and reversing all stage directions.
   You should finish facing to the front!

TRAVELLING

Good use of the floor and space is very important. The dancer can travel in all directions: forward, backward, sideways or can work 'on the spot' i.e. remain in the same place.

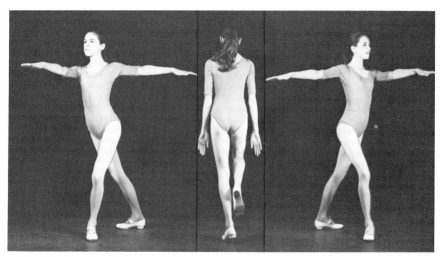

Fig. 69. Turning—¾ turn to right

TURNS

When making a ¾ or full turn, again turn away from the working foot. It will also probably be necessary to pivot (twist) on the ball of the working foot.

PICK UP

Stand with your feet slightly apart, toes turned slightly out. Turn up the toe of one foot, slap foot back sharply, striking the ground with the ball of the foot and lifting the heel. A pick up is a sharp movement giving one clear sound.

Practice
Repeat each of these exercises eight times.

(a) Hold on to a support
   &1 2   Pick up, toe tap, step R
   &3 4   Pick up, toe tap, step L

(b) &1 Pick up step travelling backwards. (As the working foot lands behind, turn up the toe of the supporting foot ready to start a pick up again.)

(c) &a1 Pick up hop step travelling backwards

(d) &a1 Pick up spring step travelling backwards.

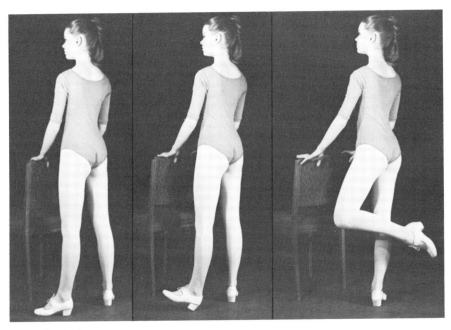

Fig. 70. Pick up

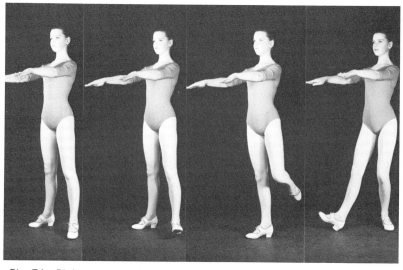

Fig. 71. Pick up step going backwards

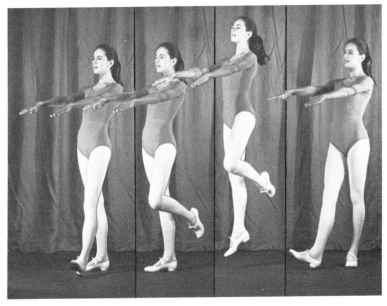

Fig. 72. Pick up hop step moving backwards

Fig. 73. Cramp roll—front view

CRAMP ROLL

Practise this with support at first.

4-beat cramp roll i.e. 4 sounds.

Raise your R foot.
Spring on to the ball of your R foot (one sound).
Step L (one sound).
Heel beat R (one sound).
Heel beat L (one sound).
These four beats are counted
     &   1   &   2

5-beat cramp roll i.e. 5 sounds.

This involves adding an extra beat to the 4-beat cramp roll and is counted &1 &a2.

&1   Tap spring R
&   Step L
a   Heel beat R
2   Heel beat L

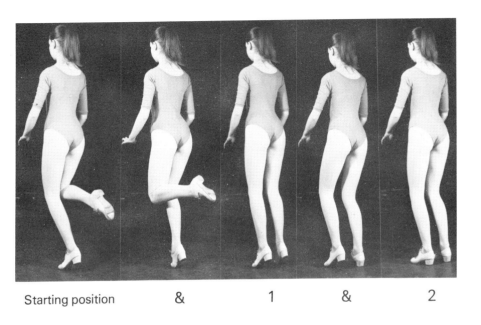

| Starting position | & | 1 | & | 2 |

Fig. 74. 4-beat cramp roll

CRAMP ROLL *Practice* Here are four 4-bar amalgamations

(a)

1		Stamp R
2		Stamp L
3		Step back R
4		Step back L
&5	&6	4-beat cramp roll, start R
&7	&8	4-beat cramp roll, start R
		Repeat.

(b)

&1	&2	Shuffle ball change R
&3	&4	4-beat cramp roll, start R
&5		Tap spring R
&6		Tap spring L
&7		Tap spring R
8		Finger snap

&1	&2	Shuffle ball change L start L
&3	&4	4-beat cramp roll start L
&5		Tap spring L
&6		Tap spring R
&7		Tap spring L
8		Finger snap

(c)

&1	&a2	5-beat cramp roll, start R
&3	&a4	5-beat cramp roll, start R
&5	6	Tap step R ball change
&7	&8	Shuffle ball change L
		Repeat starting L.

(d)

&1	&2	Tap spring toe tap hop R
&3	&4	Tap spring toe tap hop L
&5	&a6	5-beat cramp roll, start R
7		Stamp R
&8		Clap clap

Repeat starting L.

Remember: if the L foot lands first, the L heel must be grounded first in a cramp roll

STOMP

Stand on the ball of one foot, *push* the foot along the ground, finishing with a heavy heel beat and a relaxed knee.

This makes one sound.

The foot should move along the ground – look at the line in Fig. 75, and see how much the foot moves.

Practice
&1 2   Tap step R, stomp R
&3 4   Tap step L, stomp L
        Repeat three times.

Fig. 75. Stomp—finishes with heavy heel beat
(Note foot movement against line on ground)

BRUSH

Brush can be done forward or backward and gives one sound. This is a similar movement to forward and backward tap, the swing however comes from the knee and hip, and therefore the movement is broader.

Practice

Hold on to a support.

&1   Forward brush hop R
&2   Backward brush hop L
Practice eight times on each foot.

&1   Forward brush hop R
&2   Backward brush, spring on to L
Repeat three times.
Remember to land on the ball of the foot when hopping.

Fig. 76. Forward brush—a very light sound

Practice

(a) 4-bar amalgamation using stomp, brush and pick up

&1	2	Tap step stomp R
&3		Brush forward L hop R
&4		Brush backward L hop R
&5	6	Tap step stomp L
&7		Brush forward R hop L
&8		Brush backward R hop L
&1	&2	Shuffle ball change R
3		Step back R
&4		Pick up step L
&5		Pick up step R
&6		Pick up step L
&7	&8	Shuffle hop toe beat R

Use opposition and parallel arms.

(b) 4-bar amalgamation using pick ups

&1	&2	Tap step R ball change
&3	&4	Tap step L ball change
5		Step back R
&6		Pick up hop L
7		Step back L
&8		Pick up hop R
&1		Tap spring R
&2		Tap spring L
&3		Tap spring R
&4		Stamp R stamp L
&5		Pick up step L
&6		Pick up step R
&7		Ball change L
&8		Clap clap

Repeat starting L.

Fig. 77.
When you can do the
steps on your own,
try working with a
partner

SCUFF

Stand on one foot, stamp the working foot forward, carry your foot forward and off the ground. This gives one sound. The supporting knee should be slightly bent on finishing

Practice

(a)

&1	Spring on to R, to R side ball dig L
&2	Drop on to L, scuff R
&3	Backward brush R, spring R
&4	Toe tap L, hop R

Repeat starting spring on to L.

(b)

&1	Tap spring R
&2	Tap spring L
3	Stomp L
4	Scuff R
&5	Backward brush hop R
&6	Toe tap L hop R
&7 &a	Tap step R ball change
8	Scuff L

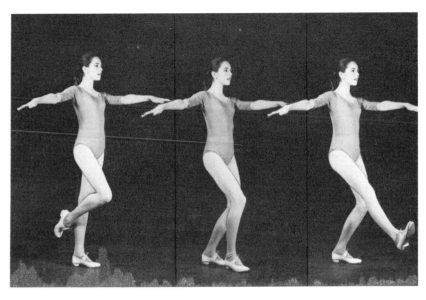

Fig. 78. Scuff—finish with supporting knee bent

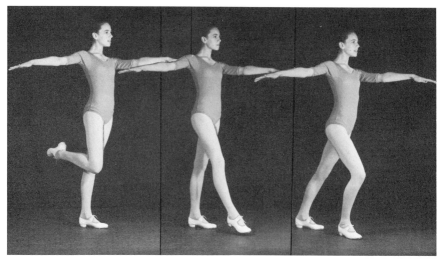

Fig. 79. Flap

FLAP

This is a forward tap followed immediately by a stamp, which gives two sounds.

Throw the foot forward: it is one continuous movement which uses the same combination as tap step, but the foot finishes flat, and the whole action is quicker.

When practising, bend your knee as the flap finishes, and make sure your heel finishes on the ground.

Practice

(a)		(b)	
&1	Tap step L	&a1	Hop R flap L
&2	Tap step R	&2	Ball change RL
&3	Flap L	&a3	Hop R flap L
&4	Flap R	&4	Ball change LR
&5	Tap step L	&5	Tap step L
&6	Tap step R	&6	Ball change RL
&7	Flap L	&7	Tap step R
&8	Flap R	&8	Ball change LR
Repeat		Repeat	

TIME STEPS

These are a series of steps performed to a steady repetitive rhythm, at an even tempo. To break up and vary the repetitive rhythm, a 'break' is used where the steps are varied slightly.

The following is an introduction to work on time steps. Always dance lightly on the balls of the feet.

Note that the phrase begins on 8&, that is, on the last beat of the bar.

SINGLE TIME STEP

Count 1 2 3 4 5 6 7

8& 1 2	Shuffle R hop L spring
&3	Tap step L forward
&	Step R beside L
4& 5 6	Shuffle L hop spring
&7	Tap step R
&	Step L beside R

SINGLE HALF BREAK i.e. half a full break

Count 1 2 3 4 5 6 7

8& 1 2	Shuffle R hop spring
&3 &	Shuffle L step
4& 5 6	Shuffle R hop spring
&7 &	Shuffle L step

A half break starts on the same foot each time
Practise this starting on the L foot.

SINGLE BREAK

Count 1 2 3 4 5 6 7

8& 1 2	Shuffle R hop spring
&3 &	Shuffle L step
4 &5	Shuffle R step
&6 &7	Shuffle L ball change
8& 1 2	Shuffle L hop spring
&3 &	Shuffle R step
4 &5	Shuffle L step
&6 &7	Shuffle R ball change

Amalgamation of single time steps:

(a) Two single time steps R foot and L
One single break
Repeat starting L foot

(b) Two single half breaks
One single break
Repeat

DOUBLE TIME STEP
This maintains the steady rhythm but adds another beat to it.

8& 1	Shuffle R hop
&2	Tap spring R
&3 &	Tap step L, step R beside
4 &5	Shuffle L hop
&6	Tap spring L
&7 &	Tap step R, step L beside

DOUBLE HALF BREAK

8& 1	Shuffle hop R
&2	Tap spring R
&3 &	Shuffle L step
4 &5	Shuffle R hop
&6	Tap spring R
&7 &	Shuffle L step

DOUBLE BREAK

8& 1	Shuffle R hop
&2	Tap spring R
&3 &	Shuffle L step
4& 5	Shuffle R step
&6	Shuffle L
&7	Ball change L

Repeat starting L
Repeat the amalgamation on page 88 using double instead of single time steps.

TRIPLE TIME STEP

8& 1	Shuffle R hop
&a2	Shuffle R spring
&3 &	Tap step L, step R beside
4 &5	Shuffle L hop
&a6	Shuffle L spring
&7 &	Tap step R, step L beside

TRIPLE HALF BREAK

8& 1	Shuffle R hop
&a 2	Shuffle R spring
&3 &	Shuffle L step
4 &5	Shuffle R hop
&a 6	Shuffle R spring
&7 &	Shuffle L step

Repeat starting L

TRIPLE BREAK

8& 1	Shuffle R hop
&a 2	Shuffle R spring
&3 &	Shuffle L step
4 &5	Shuffle R step
&6	Shuffle L
&7	Ball change L

Again, practise the amalgamations on page 88

AMALGAMATIONS

Here are three sequences using the steps you have learnt. Practise each 8-bar sequence individually until you feel confident, and then try joining them together to make a longer amalgamation

Sequence (a)
Suggested music:
'Hello Dolly', 'Stepping out with My Baby'.

&1	Tap spring R
&2	Toe tap hop L
&3	Tap spring L
&4	Toe tap hop R
&5	Tap step R
&6	Tap step L
&7 &8	Shuffle hop over (R crossing over L)
1 2	Turn completely round on the balls of your feet
3 4	Sideways jump to R and clap
&5	Spring L to L side, dig R
&6	Spring L to L side, dig R
&7	Drop on L, scuff R
&8	Step heel beat R

Repeat these four bars starting tap spring L.

Sequence (b)
Suggested music:
'On the street where You Live', 'Alexander's Ragtime Band'.

This sequence involves the use of different directions. Practise slowly at first, facing front.

&1 &2	Tap step ball change R to RDF	
&3 &4	Flap L flap R	
5	Step back L	travelling backwards to LDB
&6	Pick up step R	
&7	Pick up step L	
&8	Ball change R	
1 2	Step R, close L to R	Travelling to LDF
&3 &4	Tap step R ball change	

&5	Brush hop L
&6	Brush spring L
&7	Brush hop R
8	Brush spring R
&1 &2 3	Ball change L ball change L clap
&4 &5 &6	Ball change L ball change L clap clap
&7 8	Ball change drop to L side (R leg extended)
✗	Wait
2 3	Step R to R side, close L to R
4 &5	gallop step to R
6	Step L to L
7	Close R to L
8	Stamp L

Sequence (c)
Suggested music:
'I've got the Sun in the Morning',
'A Fella with an Umbrella'.

&1 &2	Shuffle R ball change, facing front
&3 &a4	Shuffle R ball change, stamp forward
&5 6	Tap step L stomp
&7 &8	Tap step R ball change to back
&1 &2	Shuffle L ball change
&3 &a4	Shuffle ball change L stamp
&5 6	Tap step R stomp
&7 &8	Tap step L ball change to front
&1 &2	Tap spring R toe tap hop
&3 &4	Tap spring L toe tap hop
&a5	Tap step heel beat three times turning in complete circle R
&a6	
&a7	
✗	Wait
&1 &2	Ball change L tap step to RDF
&3 &4	Tap step R ball change to LDB
5 &a6	Step back R, pick up hop step R
&a7	Pick up hop step L
8	Turn to face front

Fig. 81. Elevation—tucked jump

Fig. 80. Elevation—leap

ELEVATION

These pictures show how Elevation (or Lift) can make a dance more exciting. Jumps and leaps are used in all forms of dance, including tap.

Fig. 82. *Elevation—star jump*

Fig. 83. Elevation—leap

DUETS AND QUARTETS

It is fun working with a partner or in a group. Remember though, that dancers should complement one another, and group work should show a relationship between the dancers and not always be just two or more dancers performing the same steps at the same time.

Fig. 84. Duet

Fig. 85. Duet

Fig. 86. Duet

TACIT AND STOP TIMING

To make routines more interesting to watch and listen to, dancers use changes in tempo and rhythm, and use tacit and stop timing.

TACIT is when the music stops and only the rhythm made by the dancers' feet can be heard. A pianist usually plays the first beat of every bar, or every other bar, to help the dancers maintain the rhythm.

STOP TIMING is when the dancer stops, holding a position, and the music continues.

Fig. 87. Quartet

Now that you have read through this book and looked at the pictures you will realise what enjoyment you can have with Tap Dancing.

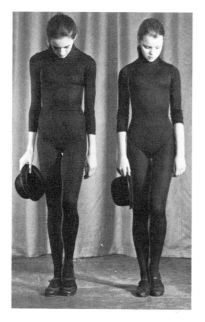

Use the book to remind you of your lessons and to practise the basic steps. Some of the elevations and modern arm lines may look rather difficult but let this encourage you to practise and practise until you become as graceful as Debbie and Sue.

Remember that you cannot expect to learn how to Tap by reading a book. If you are interested, join a local class with a good teacher to make sure you are doing the movements correctly. Then you will also find out about the possibility of obtaining medals and certificates for skill and competence awarded by the various dance Associations.